Stephen Crane

A Souvenir and Medley

Seven poems and a sketch

Stephen Crane

A Souvenir and Medley
Seven poems and a sketch

ISBN/EAN: 9783337005849

Printed in Europe, USA, Canada, Australia, Japan

Cover: Foto ©Thomas Meinert / pixelio.de

More available books at **www.hansebooks.com**

A SOUVENIR AND A MEDLEY:
SEVEN POEMS AND A SKETCH
BY
STEPHEN CRANE.
WITH DIVERS AND SUNDRY COMMUNICATIONS FROM CERTAIN EMINENT WITS.

DONE INTO PRINT
AT
THE ROYCROFT PRINTING SHOP,
WHICH IS IN EAST AURORA, N. Y.
EIGHTEEN HUNDRED AND NINETY-SIX.

I saw a man pursuing the horizon;
Round and round they sped.
I was disturbed at this;
I accosted the man.
" It is futile " I said,
" You can never —"

" You lie," he cried,
And ran on.

—The Black Riders.

CONTENTS.

FOREWORD.

On Thursday evening, Dec. 19, 1895, The Society of the Philistines gave a Dinner in honor of Mr. Stephen Crane. It was a large time, and much good copy was passed off into space that otherwise might have been used to enrich publishers.

At that time Mr. Crane's *Red Badge of Courage* was selling slowly in its second thousand. After three short months had slipped past, *The Red Badge of Courage* was outselling, both in England and the United States, any other book written by an American. It would be presumptious to claim that a single Square Meal brought such fame and fortune to a modest, blonde youth, wonderful heretofore only as a Shortstop; for it would leave the claimant the embarrassing task of proving the rate of sale that *The Red Badge* would have met with had not Mr. Crane been adopted by the Philistine Hosts and duly dined.

But the fact remains that the whirligig of time has brought a recognition of Mr. Crane's genius; and it has also brought a demand on the East Aurora colony of Philistines for a certain little Souvenir of the Dinner that was issued at the time, and which has been a deluge. To meet this demand we have printed this booklet, adding to the original text certain matter that may interest the future historian of American Letters.

FATE FROWNED UPON THEM AND THEY COULD NOT COME.

—DRYDEN.

Charles Dudley Warner.

The Crane Dinner, I hope, will encourage and strengthen the inner man without enlarging unduly that portion where our imagination is supposed to dwell.

Maurice Thompson.

It would give me great pleasure to sit over against Stephen Crane for an eating bout. Lately he made the gooseflesh wiggle on me—he is a fiendish warrior. Eat, drink and be merry! for tomorrow the critics will be abroad.

J. C. Hopper,
of the U. S. Treasury.

Mr. Crane certainly wears the Red Badge of Courage if he can face the Philistines in such an encounter as this.

Irving Bacheller.

My regards to my good friend Crane. God save his appetite for many another dinner.

Arthur Lucas,
of the Albany Express.

I have a profound admiration for a man who, casting to the winds rhyme, reason and metre, can still write poetry.

Chester S. Lord,
of the Sun.

In spirit I join you in doing honor to Mr. Crane, who is the mildest mannered man who ever cut a throat or scuttled ship (on paper).

Ripley Hitchcock.

I am glad to know that our prophets when they prove themselves such are not without honor in their own country.

Walter Storrs Bigelow,
of the Boston Commonwealth.

This is the first time I was ever asked in so fitting manner to dine with a great poet, and I am glad you have picked out so good an one as Crane.

Louise Imogen Guiney.

Miss Guiney is

> " Eycless in Gaza, at the Mill with slaves,
> Herself in bonds, (NOT) under Philistian yoke,"

and therefore is only sorry, and grateful, and absent, and sensible of a good thing and much good company missed.

Walter Blackburn Harte.

I wish Mr. Crane all good fortune in literature and life, and I trust the joy of the Philistines may be complete.

The heroism of humanity has passed forever into the hearts of those who starve and suffer and live for Literature. There is no profession holds so many true heroes—and so many damned rascals—as Literature; but Crane, who writes with the inspiration of the smell of powder, is, let us hope, first of all a Man—and afterwards a Writer.

John Langdon Heaton,
of the Recorder.

Aren't the Philistines, individually and collectively, peaches?

Ernest E. Russell,
of Public Opinion.

It will be a goodly company—and if you all slide under the table, I swear to you it will be a goodly company.

Amy Leslie,
of the Chicago News.

My most gentle thoughts are tinged with envy of you who are so lucky as to meet Stephen Crane.

Thomas W. Durston,
of Syracuse.

In December a bookseller must work days and nights and Sundays. If you will give a picnic for Crane next summer, I'll come and stay a week.

9

E. E. Winship,

of the Journal of Education.

I dote on Stephen Crane, although I don't understand his lines a bit.

Edward W. Bok.

I sincerely wish I could come, though even if I could I probably would not be able to find East Aurora. One thing is certain, you are making famous a hitherto obscure town, and that is something in these days.

Charles F. Lummis.

I am sorry that I cannot assist at the Hanging of the Crane, but I trust Justice may be done.

W. W. Campbell.

I hope the occasion may not cause too many of you to " chase the horizon " Friday morning.

Richard Harding Davis.

I will wager the dinner will be better than those you and I got in the restaurant at Creede, but I can't come. My respects to Mr. Crane.

Bliss Carman.

It would do me great pleasure to sit at feast with Mr. Crane and the bold and worthy Philistines, but I cannot find East Aurora in my Railroad Guide.

Hamlin Garland.

I take a very special interest in Mr. Crane, as I was one of the very first to know about Maggie and the Red Badge.

Mr. Cudahy.

Being engaged in writing a sequel to "The Pawns of Chance," I much regret that I cannot meet Mr. Crane at dinner. As soon as the Packing Season is over I hope to read "The Blue Badge of Bravery."

W. D. Howells.

I am very glad to know that my prophecies are being realized and that Mr. Crane is receiving recognition at a time in life when he can most enjoy it.

Robert W. Criswell,
of the Morning Advertiser.

I do not understand Crane's poetry, nor do I understand the inscription on the monolith in Central Park, but I learn from good authority that it conveys valuable information expressed in chaste and beautiful language.

(Rev.) Samuel J. Barrows,
of the Christian Register.

Although I might meet one Goliath, armed with smooth stones that I might make a hit, I dare not face a whole table of giants. Beside, the Railroads declare there is an Interstate Commerce Law, and that it is wicked to give passes.

Hayden Carruth.

I saw a Man reading an invitation.
Anon he chortled like a bull-frog—
Like a billy-be-dasted bull-frog.
It was a dinner invitation,
Which accounted for the chortle.
"They will have Grub," quoth the
Man.
"Better yet, Grape Juice, I will go!"
The red chortle died on his white lips.
His ashy hand shot into his black
Pocket.
A gray wail burst from his parched,
Brown throat
Like the scarlet yowl of a yellow
Tom Cat—
The Man didn't have the price!
Which accounted for the wail.
I left him cursing the Railroad
Company with great, jagged,
Crimson curses.

E. C. Stedman.

Judging from the vivid way in which he writes of
war, Stephen Crane must have in a former incarnation
been with the Philistines and fought for home and
native land against those marauding Children of the
Plain.

Ambrose Bierce.

Were it not for the miles which separate us, I would
be with you and lick a plate so clean that it would
not have to be washed for a month.

S. S. McClure, Limited.

I admire Mr. Crane's work, and I admire the man. I also admire the valiant Philistines—from a safe distance.

John J. Rooney.

I say advisedly that what Gœthe did for Wiemar, Shakespeare for Stratford, Whitman for Camden and Emerson for Concord, the PHILISTINE is doing for East Aurora. From the sleepy, moss-grown village, it shines forth in the bright borealis rays reflected from the burnished armor of its fierce-fighting Black Riders, and the civilized world looks on and wonders what next!

Charles S. Savage,

of G. P. Putnam's Sons.

Can't come, and it is fortunate for the Philistines that this is so, for should I come, I'd bring my Weapon and slay you all.

E. St. Elmo Lewis,

of Footlights.

To Stephen Crane we of the modern era owe much.

T. W. Higginson.

If it is really true that Crane fought through the entire Revolutionary War, taking a hand too in the Concord Fight, I can understand why his descriptions always ring true.

Daniel Appleton.

As one of the first to read and appreciate the Red Badge, I would like to be with you in honoring Mr. Crane.

L. H. Bickford,
of the Denver Times.

I should like to be present, if only for the sake of Art—for I believe in each one of the Philistines doing his best to further that Art which receives exquisite handling by Mr. Crane.

Adeline Knapp,
of the Examiner.

Say to Mr. Crane for me that the author of the Red Badge is Great People, and that, did train connections permit my reaching San Francisco before morning, more than my Astral Self were doing him honor this night.

Edward Hofer,
of the Salem (Oregon) Journal.

Accept the greeting of one in the far West who esteems it a great dignity to be called one of the brotherhood of Philistia.

George F. Warren,
of the Democrat and Chronicle.

As a poet Stephen Crane is a cracker-jack.

Geoffrey Charlton Adams.

We need such men as Crane in Gath and Askelon.

Col. John L. Burleigh.

It grieves me greatly to think I cannot be with you at the Feed. I was with Crane at Antietam and saw him rush forward, sieze two of the enemy and bump their heads together in a way that must have made them see constellations. When a Rebel General remonstrated with him, Steve, in a red fury, gave him a kick like a purple cow when all at once—but the story is too long to tell now.

AS TO THE MAN.

STEPHEN CRANE possesses genius. Just what genius is the world has not determined, for, like the ulster, the word covers a multitude of sins. But if pushed for a definition, I would say that genius is only a woman's intuition carried one step further. It is essentially feminine in its attributes, and the men of genius (as opposed to men of talent) have always been men with marked feminine qualities. The genius knows because he knows, and if you should ask the genius whence comes this power, he would answer you (if he knew) in the words of Cassius: "My mother gave it me."

Every genius has had a splendid mother. Had I space, I could name you a dozen great men—dead and gone—who were ushered into this earth-life under about the following conditions: A finely-organized, receptive, aspiring woman is thrown by fate into an unkind environment. She thirsts for knowledge, for sweet music, for beauty, for sympathy, for attainment. She has a heart-hunger that none about her comprehend; she strives for better things but those nearest her do not understand. She prays to God, but the heavens are but brass. When in this peculiar mental condition a child is born to her. This child is heir to all of his mother's spiritual desires, but he develops a man's strength and breaks the fetters that held her fast. He surmounts obstacles that she could never overcome. The woman's prayer was answered. God listened to her after all. But, like Columbus, who gave the world a continent, she dies in ignorance of what she has achieved.

Earth's buffets are usually too severe for her; she cannot endure its contumely; she goes to her long rest, soothed only by the thought that she did her work as best she could. In summer, wild flowers nod in the breeze above her forgotten grave, and in winter, the untracked snow covers with bridal white the spot where she sleeps. But far away in the gay courts of great cities the walls echo the praises of her son, and men say, Behold, a Genius!

She died that others might live. Her prayer was answered, as every sincere prayer is: for every desire of the heart has somewhere its gratification. But Nature cares not for the individual—her thought is only for the race. Do you know the history of Nancy Hanks? She is the universal type of women who give the world its men of genius.

When in 1891 Stephen Crane wrote *Maggie, a girl of the Streets*, Mr. Howells read the story, and after seeing its author said, "This man has sprung into life full-armed." And that expression of Mr. Howells' fully covers the case. I can imagine no condition of life that might entangle a man or woman within its meshes that Stephen Crane could not fully comprehend and appreciate. Men are only great as they possess sympathy. Crane knows the human heart through and through, and he sympathizes with its every pulsation. From the beggar's child searching in ash barrels for treasure, to the statesman playing at diplomacy with his chief thought on next fall's election, Stephen Crane knows the inmost soul of each and all. Whether he is able to translate it to you or not is quite another question; but in the forty or more short stories and sketches he has written I fail to find a single false note. He neither exaggerates nor comes tardy off.

The psychologists tell us that a man cannot fully comprehend a condition that he has never experienced. But theosophy explains the transcendent wisdom of genius by saying that in former incarnations the man passed through these experiences. Emerson says: "We are bathed in an ocean of intelligence, and under right conditions the soul knows all things." These things may be true, but the secret of Crane's masterly delineation is that he is able to project himself into the condition of others.

He does not describe men and women—*he is that man.* He loses his identity, forgets self, abandons his own consciousness, and is for the moment the individual who speaks. And whether this individual is man, woman or child, makes no difference. Sex, age, condition, weigh not in the scale.

During the latter half of the year 1895 no writing man in America was so thoroughly hooted and so well abused as Stephen Crane. I have a scrap-book of newspaper clippings that is a symposium of Billingsgate mud-balls, with Crane for the target. Turning the leaves of this scrap-book I find used in reference to a plain little book called *The Black Riders*, these words: Idiocy, drivel, bombast, rot, nonsense, puerility, untruth, garbage, hamfat, funny, absurd, childish, drunken, besotted, obscure, opium-laden, blasphemous, indecent, fustian, rant, bassoon-poetry, swell-head stuff, bluster, balderdash, windy, turgid, stupid, pompous, gasconade, gas-house ballads, etc., etc.

There are also in this scrap-book upward of a hundred parodies on the poems. Some of these are rather clever, but they differ from Crane's work in this, that there is not a molecule of thought in one of them, while there is a great moral truth taught in each of Crane's poems. It's so easy to write a parody; a parody is a calico cat stuffed with cotton; it pleases the little boys who wear dresses. Usually, people—even sensible people—will not take time to find it. But one might as well accuse Æsop of idiocy when he has a fox talk to a goose. Of course, we could truthfully swear that no fox ever carried on a conversation with a goose since the world began. But to assume that Æsop was therefore a fool would be proof that the man who made the assumption was a fool and not Æsop.

The "Lines" in *The Black Riders* seem to me very wonderful : charged with meaning like a storage battery. But there is a fine defy in the flavour that warns the reader not to take too much or it may strike in. Who wants a meal of horseradish? When I hear intelligent people jeer at *The Black Riders* (and intelligent people do jeer at *The Black Riders*) I think of those Chicago hand-me-out restaurants where men woo dyspepsia, (and win the termagent) fighting like crimson devils for pie, and gulp things red hot because Time and the Stock Exchange wait for no man ; or perhaps of Paul Bourget who swallowed three fingers of Worcestershire Sauce on a Pullman Dining Car and then made a memorandum in his note book that American wines are very bad.

Any man who has a tuppence worth of philosophy in his clay, and a little of God's leisure at his disposal that will allow him to take his mental aliment with pulse at normal, will find a good honest nugget of wisdom in every sentence of Copeland & Day's unique little work. Yet I admit that in a certain mood the brevity of expression is rather exasperating, and the independence of spirit which shows that the author can do without *you* is the quip modest, if not the reproof valiant, that is not always pleasant. But granting that there are some things in *The Black Riders* that I do not especially like, I yet have no quarrel with the book. I accept it and give thanks.

But granting for argument's sake that *The Black Riders* is "rot," it then must be admitted that it was a great stroke of worldly wisdom. For Stephen Crane now has the ear of the world. Publishers besiege him with checks in advance, and the manuscript of a story he has just completed has been bid on by four different firms, with special offers for the English copyright. Tradition has it that the sixty-eight short poems in *The Black Riders* were all written in the space of two days and a night—in a time of terrible depression. The work was then handed to a dear friend. This friend thought he saw the deep burning thought of a prophet in the lines, and he conceived the plan of publishing them. A thousand copies were printed and sold inside of six months. If you want a first edition of *The Black Riders* now, it will cost you five dollars, and if you can pick up a *Maggie of the Streets* for twice that, you'd better do it—and do it quick.

Stephen Crane attended Lafayette College for a time in his nineteenth year. The teachers there write me that they remember him only as "a yellow, tow-haired youth, who would rather fight than study."

They advised him to "take a change," so he went to Syracuse University—his guardian being anxious he should be "educated." His fame at Syracuse rests on the fact that he was the best short-stop ever on the University baseball team. He soon became captain, this on account of his ability to hold his own when it came to an issue with certain "scrapping" antagonists.

Once when he was called upon to recite in the psychology class, he argued a point with the teacher. The Professor sought to silence him by an appeal to the Bible: "Tut, tut—what does St. Paul say, Mr. Crane, what does St. Paul say?" testily asked the old Professor.

"I know what St. Paul says," was the answer, "but I disagree with St. Paul."

Of course no Methodist college wants a student like that; and young Crane wandered down to New York and got a job reporting on the *Herald*.

Since then he has worked on the editorial staff of various papers. He is now, however, devoting his whole time to letters, living at Hartwood, Sullivan County, N. Y. Hartwood has a store, a blacksmith shop and a tavern. When the train comes in all of the citizens go down to the station to see 'er go through. Should you ask one of these citizens who Stephen Crane is, he would probably answer you as he did me:

"Mr. Crane, Mr. Crane! you mean Steve Crane?

" Yes."

" Why, he's—he's Steve Crane an' a dern good feller ! "

Mr. Crane is now in his twenty-fifth year. He is a little under the average height, and is slender and slight in build, weighing scarcely one hundred and thirty pounds. He is a decided blonde : his eyes blue. His intellect is as wide awake as the matin chimes, and his generosity is as ample as the double chin of Col. Ingersoll. His handsome, boyish face and quiet, half-shy, modest manner make him a general favorite everywhere with women. And to me, it is rather curious that women should flock around and pet this sort of a man, who can read their inmost thoughts just as that Roentgen invention can photograph things inside of a box, when a big, stupid man with a red face and a black mustache they are very much afraid of.

At a recent banquet given by the Society of the Philistines, in honor of Mr. Crane, thirty-one men sat at the feast. These men had come from Chicago, New York, Boston, and elsewhere to attend the dinner. Several lawyers, one eminent physician, and various writers were there. Crane was the youngest individual at the board, but he showed himself the peer of any man present. His speech was earnest, dignified, yet modestly expressed. His manner is singularly well poised, and his few words carry conviction.

Still he can laugh and joke, and no man has a better appreciation of humor. He loves the out-doors, and in riding horseback by his side across country I have admired his happy abandon, as he sits secure, riding with loose rein and long stirrup in a reckless rush.

In the New York *Times* for January 26 is a two-column letter from London, by that distinguished critic, Mr. Harold Frederic. The subject of the entire article is Stephen Crane. Says Mr. Frederic:

"The 'Red Badge of Courage' appeared a couple of months ago, unheralded and unnoticed, in a series which, under the distinctive label of 'Pioneer,' is popularly supposed to present fiction more or less after the order of 'The Green Carnation,' which was also of that lot. The first one who mentioned in my hearing that this 'Red Badge' was well worth reading happened to be a person whose literary admirations serve me generally as warnings what to avoid, and I remembered the title languidly from that standpoint of self-protection. A little later others began to speak of it. All at once, every bookish person had it at his tongue's end. It was clearly a book to read, and I read it. Even as I did so, reviews burst forth in a dozen different quarters, hailing it as extraordinary. Some were naturally more excited and voluble than others, but all the critics showed, and continue to show, their sense of being in the presence of something not like other things.

24

George Wyndham, M. P., has already written of it in *The New Review* as 'a remarkable book.' Other magazine editors have articles about it in preparation, and it is evident that for the next few months it is to be more talked about than anything else in current literature. It seems almost equally certain that it will be kept alive, as one of the deathless books which must be read by everybody who desires to be, or to seem a connoisseur of modern fiction.

"If there were in existence any books of a similar character, one could start confidently by saying it was the best of its kind. But it has no fellows. It is a book outside of all classification. So unlike anything else is it, that the temptation rises to deny that it is a book at all. When one searches for comparisons, they can only be found by culling out selected portions from the trunks of masterpieces, and considering these detached fragments, one by one, with reference to the 'Red Badge,' which is itself a fragment, and yet is complete. Thus one lifts the best battle pictures from Tolstoi's great 'War and Peace,' from Balzacs 'Chouans,' from Hugo's 'Les Miserables,' and the forest fight in ''93,' from Prosper Merimee's 'Assault of the Redoubt,' from Zola's 'La Debacle' and 'Attack on the Mill' (it is strange enough that equivalents in the literature of our own language do not suggest themselves), and studies them side by side with this tremendously effective battle painting by the unknown youngster. Positively they are cold and ineffectual beside it. The praise may sound exaggerated, but really it is inadequate. These renowned battle descriptions of the big men are made to seem all wrong. The 'Red Badge' impels the feeling that the actual truth about a battle has never been guessed before."

There is a class of reviewers who always wind up their preachments by saying: "This book gives much promise, and we shall look anxiously for Mr. Scribbler's next." Let us deal in no such cant. A man's work is good or it is not. As for his "next," nobody can tell whether it will be good or not. There is a whole army of men about to do something great, but the years go by and they never do it. They are like those precocious children who stand on chairs and recite "pieces." They never make orators. As to Crane's "future work," let us keep silent. But if he never produces another thing, he has done enough to save the fag-end of the century from literary disgrace; and look you, friends, that is no small matter !

E. H. in *The Lotos*.

THE CHATTER OF A DEATH-DEMON FROM A TREE-
    TOP.

BLOOD—BLOOD AND TORN GRASS—
HAD MARKED THE RISE OF HIS AGONY—
THIS LONE HUNTER,
THE GREY-GREEN WOODS IMPASSIVE
HAD WATCHED THE THRESHING OF HIS LIMBS.

A CANOE WITH FLASHING PADDLE,
A GIRL WITH SOFT, SEARCHING EYES,
A CALL: "JOHN!"

*   *   *   *   *   *   *   *   *   *

COME, ARISE, HUNTER!
LIFT YOUR GREY FACE!
CAN YOU NOT HEAR?

THE CHATTER OF A DEATH-DEMON FROM A TREE-
    TOP.

EACH SMALL GLEAM WAS A VOICE
—A LANTERN VOICE—
IN LITTLE SONGS OF CARMINE, VIOLET, GREEN,
    GOLD.
A CHORUS OF COLORS CAME OVER THE WATER,
THE WONDROUS LEAF-SHADOWS NO LONGER WAV-
    ERED,
NO PINES CROONED ON THE HILLS,
THE BLUE NIGHT WAS ELSEWHERE A SILENCE
WHEN THE CHORUS OF COLORS CAME OVER THE
    WATER,
LITTLE SONGS OF CARMINE, VIOLET, GREEN, GOLD.
SMALL GLOWING PEBBLES
THROWN ON THE DARK PLANE OF EVENING
SING GOOD BALLADS OF GOD
AND ETERNITY, WITH SOUL'S REST.
LITTLE PRIESTS, LITTLE HOLY FATHERS,
NONE CAN DOUBT THE TRUTH OF YOUR HYMNING
WHEN THE MARVELOUS CHORUS COMES OVER THE
    WATER,
SONGS OF CARMINE, VIOLET, GREEN, GOLD.

A SLANT OF SUN ON DULL BROWN WALLS
A FORGOTTEN SKY OF BASHFUL BLUE.

TOWARD GOD A MIGHTY HYMN
A SONG OF CLASHES AND CRIES,
RUMBLING WHEELS, HOOF-BEATS, BELLS,
WELCOMES, FAREWELLS, LOVE-CALLS, FINAL
    MOANS,
VOICES OF JOY, IDIOCY, WARNING, DESPAIR,
THE UNKNOWN APPEALS OF BRUTES,
THE CHANTING OF VIOLETS,
THE SCREAMS OF CUT TREES,
THE SENSELESS BABBLE OF HENS AND WISE MEN—
A CLUTTERED INCOHERENCY THAT SAYS AT THE
    STARS:
" O, GOD SAVE US !"

"I HAVE HEARD THE SUNSET SONG OF THE BIRCHES
"A WHITE MELODY IN THE SILENCE.
"I HAVE SEEN A QUARREL OF THE PINES.
"AT NIGHTFALL,
"THE LITTLE GRASSES HAVE RUSHED BY ME
"WITH THE WIND-MEN.
"THESE THINGS HAVE I LIVED," QUOTH THE MANIAC
"POSSESSING ONLY EYES AND EARS.
"BUT, YOU—
"YOU DON GREEN SPECTACLES BEFORE YOU LOOK AT ROSES."

" WHAT SAYS THE SEA, LITTLE SHELL?
" WHAT SAYS THE SEA?
" LONG HAS OUR BROTHER BEEN SILENT TO US,
" KEPT HIS MESSAGE FOR THE SHIPS,
" AWKWARD SHIPS, STUPID SHIPS."

" THE SEA BIDS YOU MOURN, OH, PINES,
" SING LOW IN THE MOONLIGHT.
" HE SENDS TALE OF THE LAND OF DOOM,
" OF PLACE WHERE ENDLESS FALLS
" A RAIN OF WOMEN'S TEARS.
" AND MEN IN GREY ROBES—
" MEN IN GREY ROBES—
" CHANT THE UNKNOWN PAIN."

" WHAT SAYS THE SEA, LITTLE SHELL?
" WHAT SAYS THE SEA?
" LONG HAS OUR BROTHER BEEN SILENT TO US,
" KEPT HIS MESSAGE FOR THE SHIPS,
" PUNY SHIPS, SILLY SHIPS."

" THE SEA BIDS YOU TEACH, OH, PINES,
" SING LOW IN THE MOONLIGHT,
" TEACH THE GOLD OF PATIENCE,
" CRY GOSPEL OF GENTLE HANDS,
" CRY A BROTHERHOOD OF HEARTS,
" THE SEA BIDS YOU TEACH, OH, PINES."

" AND WHERE IS THE REWARD, LITTLE SHELL?
" WHAT SAYS THE SEA?
" LONG HAS OUR BROTHER BEEN SILENT TO US,
" KEPT HIS MESSAGE FOR THE SHIPS,
" PUNY SHIPS, SILLY SHIPS."

" NO WORD SAYS THE SEA, OH, PINES,
" NO WORD SAYS THE SEA.
" LONG WILL YOUR BROTHER BE SILENT TO YOU,
" KEEP HIS MESSAGE FOR THE SHIPS,
" OH, PUNY PINES, SILLY PINES."

TO THE MAIDEN
THE SEA WAS BLUE MEADOW
ALIVE WITH LITTLE FROTH-PEOPLE
SINGING.

TO THE SAILOR, WRECKED,
THE SEA WAS DEAD GREY WALLS
SUPERLATIVE IN VACANCY
UPON WHICH NEVERTHELESS AT FATEFUL TIME,
WAS WRITTEN
THE GRIM HATRED OF NATURE.

FAST RODE THE KNIGHT
WITH SPURS, HOT AND REEKING
EVER WAVING AN EAGER SWORD.
" TO SAVE MY LADY ! "
FAST RODE THE KNIGHT
AND LEAPED FROM SADDLE TO WAR.
MEN OF STEEL FLICKERED AND GLEAMED
LIKE RIOT OF SILVER LIGHTS
AND THE GOLD OF THE KNIGHTS GOOD BANNER
STILL WAVED ON A CASTLE WALL.
    *   *   *   *   *   *   *   *   *   *

A HORSE
BLOWING, STAGGERING, BLOODY THING
FORGOTTEN AT FOOT OF CASTLE WALL.
A HORSE
DEAD AT FOOT OF CASTLE WALL.

A GREAT MISTAKE.

AN ITALIAN kept a fruit stand on a corner where he had good aim at the people who came down from the elevated station and at those who went along two thronged streets. He sat most of the day in a backless chair that was placed strategically.

There was a babe living hard by, up five flights of stairs, who regarded this Italian as a tremendous being. The babe had investigated this fruit stand. It had thrilled him as few things he had met with in his travels had thrilled him. The sweets of the world laid there in dazzling rows, tumbled in luxurious heaps. When he gazed at this Italian seated amid such splendid treasure, his lower lip hung low and his eyes raised to the vendor's face were filled with deep respect, worship, as if he saw omnipotence.

The babe came often to this corner. He hovered

about the stand and watched each detail of the business. He was fascinated by the tranquility of the vendor, the majesty of power and possession. At times, he was so engrossed in his contemplation that people, hurrying, had to use care to avoid bumping him down.

He had never ventured very near to the stand. It was his habit to hang warily about the curb. Even there he resembled a babe who looks unbidden at a feast of gods.

One day, however, as the baby was thus staring, the vendor arose and going along the front of the stand, began to polish oranges with a red pocket-handkerchief. The breathless spectator moved across the sidewalk until his small face almost touched the vendor's sleeve. His fingers were gripped in a fold of his dress.

At last, the Italian finished with the oranges and returned to his chair. He drew a newspaper printed in his language from behind a bunch of bananas. He settled himself in a comfortable position and began to glare savagely at the print. The babe was left face to face with the massed joys of the world.

For a time he was a simple worshipper at this golden shrine. Then tumultuous desires began to shake him. His dreams were of conquest. His lips moved. Presently into his head there came a little plan.

He sidled nearer, throwing swift and cunning

35

glances at the Italian. He strove to maintain his conventional manner, but the whole plot was written upon his countenance.

At last he had come near enough to touch the fruit. From the tattered skirt came slowly his small dirty hand. His eyes were still fixed upon the vendor. His features were set, save for the under lip, which had a faint fluttering movement. The hand went forward.

Elevated trains thundered to the station and the stairway poured people upon the sidewalks. There was a deep sea roar from feet and wheels going ceaselessly. None seemed to perceive the babe engaged in the great venture.

The Italian turned his paper. Sudden panic smote the babe. His hand dropped and he gave vent to a cry of dismay. He remained for a moment staring at the vendor. There was evidently a great debate in his mind. His infant intellect had defined the Italian. The latter was undoubtedly a man who would eat babes that provoked him. And the alarm in him when the vendor had turned his newspaper brought vividly before him the consequences if he were detected.

But at this moment, the vendor gave a blissful grunt and tilting his chair against a wall, closed his eyes. His paper dropped unheeded.

The babe ceased his scrutiny and again raised his hand. It was moved with supreme caution toward the fruit. The fingers were bent, claw-like, in the manner of great heart-shaking greed.

Once he stopped and chattered convulsively because the vendor moved in his sleep. The babe with his eyes still upon the Italian again put forth his hand and the rapacious finger closed over a round bulb.

And it was written that the Italian should at this moment open his eyes. He glared at the babe a fierce question. Thereupon the babe thrust the round bulb behind him and with a face expressive of the deepest guilt, began a wild but elaborate series of gestures declaring his innocence.

The Italian howled. He sprang to his feet, and with three steps overtook the babe. He whirled him fiercely and took from the little fingers a lemon.

STEPHEN CRANE.

A PROLOGUE.

A GLOOMY STAGE. SLENDER CURTAINS AT A WINDOW, CENTRE. BEFORE THE WINDOW, A TABLE, AND UPON THE TABLE, A LARGE BOOK, OPENED. A MOONBEAM, NO WIDER THAN A SWORD-BLADE, PIERCES THE CURTAINS AND FALLS UPON THE BOOK.

A MOMENT OF SILENCE.

FROM WITHOUT, THEN—AN ADJACENT ROOM IN INTENTION—COME SOUNDS OF CELEBRATION, OF RIOTOUS DRINKING AND LAUGHTER. FINALLY, A SWIFT QUARREL. THE DIN AND CRASH OF A FIGHT. A LITTLE STILLNESS. THEN A WOMAN'S SCREAM. " AH, MY SON, MY SON."

A MOMENT OF SILENCE.

CURTAIN.

STEPHEN CRANE.

SOME HISTORICAL DOCUMENTS.

There has been an entertaining aftermath of the dinner which the Society of the Philistines gave to Mr. Stephen Crane, who wears a red badge for his black riding. It consists of a pamphlet containing the words of regret sent to the committee in charge by distinguished workers in the literary vineyard. It is evident that many prominent gentlemen who would have enjoyed grasping Mr. Crane by the hand did not find it quite so easy to make a little journey to East Aurora, N. Y., as Mr. Elbert Hubbard has found it. Mr. Bok could not find the town, Bliss Carman says it is not in his railroad guide, and Philistines from San Francisco found it impossible to make train connections. But they all joined in the spirit of the festival, and all toasted the hanging of the Crane.

Even in these notes of regret we can see a great diversity of opinion in regard to Mr. Crane's contributions to our literature. It is a delicate task to say in a letter answering an invitation to dinner that you do not understand what the author in whose honor it is to be given means by his work. But some brave men did this brave thing. Charles Dudley Warner simply wished the inner man a good time; Maurice Thompson said Crane was a fiendish warrior who made his gooseflesh wiggle; Miss Louise Imogen Guiney knew she was missing a " good thing ; " Richard Harding Davis avoided criticising the poet in question by wagering it would be a better dinner than he had eaten at Creede; Hamlin Garland vouched for his taking " a very special interest in Mr. Crane ; " Mr. Howells was glad his prophecies were being realized, and that one man is receiving recognition at a time in life when he can most enjoy it, recognition in this instance being food, varied with Sauterne, St. Julian and Irroy ; and other authors replied in a similar strain.

On the other hand, a genius from Albany wrote : " I have a profound admiration for a man who, casting to the winds rhyme, reason and metre, can still write poetry." A Boston educator said : " I dote on Stephen Crane, although I don't understand his lines a bit." But more pat than any other message was that sent to East Aurora by a New York newspaper man, who said he did not understand Crane's poetry, nor did he understand the monolith in Central Park, although he had learned from good authority that " it conveys valuable information, expressed in chaste and beautiful language."—*The Boston Journal.*

To the younger generation of book lovers a great deal of interest and not a little curiosity have lately been excited by the achievements of that new stellar light in the twinkling dome of American letters, Mr. Stephen Crane. Their introduction to him has been recent. Some poetry that, while violating with serene self-confidence well-nigh all the traditions and conventions of versification, nevertheless spoke forth a virile message, deep in its philosophy, daring in its imagery and unmistakable in the subtle play of its writer's genius; this and a strange performance in prose comprise about all that the majority of ordinarily informed readers yet know concerning Stephen Crane. To be sure, some of them have heard, in a faint way, that he is a young author whose future is brilliant with high promise. Mr. Howells has said as much. Mr. E. J. Edwards, the reviewer and correspondent, has frequently reiterated the statement; and in New York, within the partly coincident circles of journalism and letters, several persons of equal or less renown have undertaken in a modest way to act as Mentors to the young genius and to aid in " bringing him out." But to the mass, he is known, if at all, only as the author of *The Black Riders* in verse, and of the *Red Badge of Courage* in prose; efforts, both, that challenge study and baffle understanding rather than soothe superficiality or pander to the wishes of mental indolence.

In these two works, and especially in the prose one, there existed a quality which, among the curious, courted investigation. To those who knew that these strong, strange writings, these bold reachings into the depths of nature and of truth, were the achievements of a boy scarcely beyond his majority —of a lad who at 17 had placed pen upon paper with the confidence and in some degree with the warrant of well-seasoned maturity—they amounted to a piquant challenge. Some there were who felt it a duty to extend the hand of fraternal recognition; and a pleasure to make of this duty a chance for personal scrutiny and for study at short range. No doubt it was this motive which inspired the Society of the Philistines, an organization of bright newspaper and literary workers which has its axis about East Aurora, N. Y., the home of *The Philistine* magazine, to scheme the emprise of a dinner to Mr. Crane, the consummation of which was pleasantly commemorated. The dinner itself was an exquisite effect in artistic gustatation; but it was chiefly notable as an incident in the early career of a possible immortal, and perchance as a refutation of the dictum that no good thing can come out of Judea. There were present at it representative bright minds in letters, in journalism, in medicine, in the law, in architecture, and in the art which speaks through colors, not to mention a liberal sprinkling of men who practice the less ethereal art of practical business; and these men, one and all, extolled what Mr. Crane had done, urged that he remain true to the best instincts within him, and pleaded for room and recognition for the newer generation of writers who aim to speak a true thought in a way not cramped by the archaic conventions.

In this personal age, to speak of an achievement inevitably incurs the complementary duty of exploiting a personality. There is little to be said of Stephen Crane, the individual, further than that he is a youthful-looking, modest person, with a face that suggests at once strong mentality and supersensitive nerves; and with a manner that shows no signs of spoiling. He is now 24 years of age, although he looks a year or two older. The *Red Badge of Courage* was begun ere he was 18 and finished before its author had become a voter. An oracular English reviewer of it the other day, in a pretentious Anglican quarterly, expatiated at some length upon the book's internal evidence that the writer of it had expressed his own emotions as a soldier bearing arms; whereas, Mr.

Crane had probably never smelled even the gun-powder of sham battle prior to the book's accept-ance by the Appleton's. Mr. Crane has been at in-tervals in active newspaper harness. He is one of the craft, and is thoroughly one with it in its sympa-thies and ideals.

Although the temptation is before him to work fast and carelessly, in order that the financial crop of his popularity may be harvested at its seeming ripeness, he refuses to pot-boil; and firm friends are sustain-ing him in it. The *Red Badge of Courage* has fas-cinated England. The critics are wild over it, and the English edition has been purchased with avidity. Mr. Crane has letters from the most prominent of English publishers asking for the English rights to all of his future productions; but the young author re-fuses to be hurried. "I write what is in me," he said, at the Square Meal, "and it will be enough to follow with obedience the promptness of that inspir-ation if it be worthy of so dignified a name."— *Liv S. Richard in the Scranton Tribune.*

The Philistine dinner in honor of Stephen Crane was no joke after all. It was given on December 19th, although East Aurora is to be found nowhere in the railway guide. Thirty-one Philistines of the sterner sex sat 'round the festal board. Miss Louise Imogen Guiney could not come, hence her regrets, printed on the menu:

Eyeless in Gaza, at the mill with slaves,
Herself in bonds, (not) under Philistian yoke.

It was a regular Clover Club affair, and many be-gan asking, "Who is Stephen Crane?" while others present echoed the sentiment of A. E. Winship, who was unavoidably absent, "I dote on Stephen Crane, although I don't understand his lines a bit." Dwight R. Collin's design for the menu represented the Black Riders and the man chasing the horizon. In the same spirit several sent regrets. Maurice Thompson said it would have given him "great pleasure to sit over against Stephen Crane for an eating bout. Lately he made the goose-flesh wiggle on me—he is a fiendish warrior." Charles F. Lummis was sorry that he could not "assist at the Hanging of the Crane." W. D. Howells was very glad to know that his "prophecies were being realized." Robert W. Criswell did not "understand Crane's poetry, nor do I understand the inscription on the monolith in Central Park." George F. Warren said that "as a poet Stephen Crane is a cracker-jack."

Several of those who did accept, with the understanding that they need not "talk" to the Philistines, were assured that they would be ready to talk after the fourth course. And so it was; everybody talked. But first Elbert Hubbard, in a very neat and humorous speech, made the address of welcome, explained the modern meaning of the word "Philistine," and likewise the object and purpose of the society. The Philistines had always had a hard time since first driven out of their country by a tribe of invaders who had been slaves in Egypt, and "had the pull with the publishers." His vindication of the apostles of sincerity and personal independence was convincing and conclusive, and he closed with an eloquent tribute to the "strong voice now heard in America, the voice of Stephen Crane." The Master of Ceremonies here winked slyly at the guest of honor at his right, and the spare, pale-faced young man, who may be twenty-five or under, and whose appearance recalled Henley's line,

"Thin-legged, thin-chested, slight unspeakably,"

found his feet and modestly acknowledged the tribute paid him by the society. He said he was trying to do what he could " since he had recovered from college," sincerely, though clumsily, perhaps, to set forth his impressions. The machinery given him might be defective, but, such as it was, it seemed his duty to work it for what it was worth. Mr. Crane's speech would read something like one of his poems, and all the time he was delivering it one was thinking of the words Edward FitzGerald asked should be inscribed on his tomb:

"It is He that hath made us, and not we ourselves."

The toast master said that the author having unfolded his plan of work, it was now the typefounder's turn, but the story of this speaker was so full of typographical errors that the Philistines rung him down and called for the paper-maker. This was a sort of machine-made affair with deckle edges and no gilt on, and in due time the publisher was asked to tell what he had to say to the Philistines that might be new and interesting about book-making. But the publisher had done little else during his six months of business experience than to read *Little Journeys*, *The Philistine*, and rejected manuscripts. He was assured there was some phosphorous in his speech, but as the diners had passed the fourth course he thought the sparkle was all in the champagne. A reviewer, the editor of *Brains*, Willis Hawkins, followed, but he was not allowed to finish his story. The censor of the occasion, Claude F. Bragdon, told how the Philistines were trying in art to stimulate and cultivate sincerity of expression, and with a keen sense of humor depicted the serious pretensions of some of the old masters and their worshipers. There were many other informal addresses, interlarded with "asides" from the wits, and much drinking of healths and successes, which extended well into the night, when the diners lapsed into solemnity long enough to enable the toast master to propose adjournment with a toast to "the first of American newspaper-men"—Charles Anderson Dana. It was a large and happy time and will long be remembered by those present.—*W. Irving Way in Chicago Post.*

A MOUNTAIN WOMAN. By ELIA W. PEAT-
TIE. With cover design by Mr. Bruce Rogers.
16mo, cloth, gilt top, $1.25.

The author of "A Mountain Woman" is an editorial writer on the Omaha *World-Herald*, and is
widely known in the Middle West as a writer of a
number of tales of Western life that are characterized
by much finish and charm.

THE LAMP OF GOLD. By FLORENCE L.
SNOW, President of the Kansas Academy of Language and Literature. Printed at the De Vinne
Press on French hand-made paper. With title-
page and cover designs by Mr. Edmund H. Gar-
rett. 16mo, cloth, gilt top, $1.25.

PURCELL ODE AND OTHER POEMS. By
ROBERT BRIDGES. 16mo, cloth, gilt top, $1.25
net.

Two hundred copies printed on Van Gelder hand-
made paper for sale in America.

HAND AND SOUL. By DANTE GABRIEL ROS-
SETTI. Printed by Mr. William Morris at the
Kelmscott Press.

This book is printed in the "Golden" type, with
a specially designed title-page and border, and in
special binding. "Hand and Soul" first appeared
in "The Germ," the short-lived magazine of the
Pre-Raphælite Brotherhood. A few copies remain
for sale at $3.50. Vellum copies all sold.

*For sale by all booksellers, or mailed postpaid by the
publishers, on receipt of price.*

WAY & WILLIAMS,
Monadnock Block.   Chicago.

48

www.ingramcontent.com/pod-product-compliance
Lightning Source LLC
Chambersburg PA
CBHW032120080426
42733CB00008B/996